I0799062

Andy Lee

by Jennifer Jacobson
illustrated by Jon Agee

Core Decodable 114

McGraw Hill Education

Bothell, WA • Chicago, IL • Columbus, OH • New York, NY

MHEonline.com

Send all inquiries to:
McGraw-Hill Education
8787 Orion Place
Columbus, OH 43240

ISBN: 978-0-02-140698-2
MHID: 0-02-140698-7

Printed in the United States of America.

7 8 9 LCR 25 24 23

Andy Lee the Timid

Andy Lee was a timid man. He was also an artist and made stained glass windows. His glass made rainbows dance in rooms.

One day, Andy made a window pane for an inn. He took the window pane to an inn that was far away. Timid Andy walked and walked.

Andy came to the town where the inn was. Down the street ran a maid.

"Turn back!" she cried. "Do not go! A chair is knocking. Drapes are swaying. It's dark and awful in that inn!"

"Stay with me," whispered timid Andy.

Andy and the maid came to a gate.

Out ran a cook waving a spoon.

"Turn back!" cried the cook. "A chair is knocking. Drapes are swaying. A tablecloth is floating. It's dark and scary in there!"

"Stay with me," whispered timid Andy.

Andy Lee the Brave

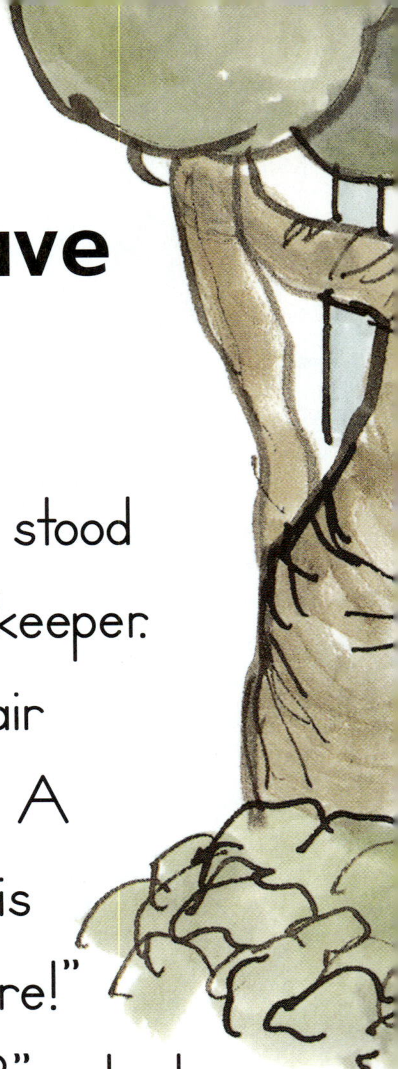

Andy, the maid, and the cook stood at the entrance. Out ran an innkeeper.

"Turn back!" she cried. "A chair is knocking. Drapes are swaying. A tablecloth is floating, and a hat is tipping. It's dark and scary in here!"

"But what about the window?" asked Andy. "I am a timid man, but this is my best window ever. I will still put in my window."

INN

Timid Andy walked in. It was dark and scary. A chair was knocking, drapes were swaying, a tablecloth was floating, and a hat was tipping.

Andy felt a breeze. He found a broken window. He put in the new window. It fit perfectly.

Andy turned around. The chair was not knocking, and drapes were not swaying. The tablecloth was not floating. The hat was not tipping. It was not dark and scary in there. Rainbows danced in the room.

Andy was an artist. His glass made rainbows dance in rooms. It also made him brave.